Bones

Bones

By: Jessica Lyon-Wall

Illustrator: Autumn Lilith Faye

Seed Royale Publishing

For Ben, who waited for me underneath the stars.

CONTENTS

CONTENTS

"The Craft"
I chose my craft but was not
Created in its image.
I wasn't allowed at 5 to float and dive
In a pretty pink leotard.
I was sickly.
I had no hips and
Though I dreamt of
Swan-like arms and swollen feet,
It wasn't supposed to be.

The scars (the first ones) reeked of sour milk
Things burst that shouldn't
explode.
I didn't choose that.
Scars, the afterwards,
I wrote them on myself,
The colour of the fruit.
Said little but
Raided the piggy bank,
Then moved to the tune of their gilded frames.

I dabbled in my teenage years
and starved myself to fit.

BY: JESSICA LYON-WALL

It took me in and held me
Carefully as a butterfly,
I emerged, but my bones sang.

At 18 when it hurt too much,
Disease bled me dry.
I danced at clubs
Instead,
Above the waist of my crutches
Or chair.

No.
Now I just watch and wait.
All I can say is, read my epitaph.
I've breathed life into words, but-
I used to dance.

"Beneath the Blonde"
Breaking out of glitter and gold,
I throw myself into the folds
Of pillows, soft, I lie and weep-
Maidens will, yet I cannot sleep.

Red roses at the monstrous door,
I live for the boys I knew before,
When they leave, I breathe too deep-
Maidens will, yet I cannot sleep.

It's the only thing that can be done,
Just greasy waves and boundless sun,
But, oh!
The promises I keep-
Maidens will, yet I cannot sleep.

BY: JESSICA LYON-WALL

"When I Fall Asleep"

I was 12 when they brought me back.
The process
Was a slow one,
Over a year I went unnoticed,
Pale, thin, and guzzling
My brother's juice in secret,
For fear of getting caught.

One day I went to sleep
And didn't wake up.
I don't know how I got there,
But I remember some bright lights.
Then starched sheets and my teddy,
The wires in my hair.
They said I had been done 3 days,
Link up my machines,
I could be an industry!

(This is perhaps a story I should never tell)

I'd find my mum in the medicine room,
Practicing,
Stabbing citrus again,
But oranges don't bruise and satsumas
Don't feel pain.

The needles get shorter,
The technology refined.
They were ever sure
They would fix chemistry in my lifetime,
And find a decent cure.

I am fearful, and alone with it.

That is how it feels.

And if I do sleep,
I have the dreams.

I settle down,
I pull the duvet up,
Turn the lamp off,
I wonder what my night will bring,
Whether my body is done,
If the morning will come.
Or if it will blossom
Into the perfect combination
Of sugar and hormones,
A day I've never seen before.
At the clock's twelfth strike,
Now the sun glows
Like corridor lights.

How I live is this-
And this is what it's like.

BY: JESSICA LYON-WALL

"Harm"

The devil's in the details
(So they say)
You don't recall very much,
As I recall,
The still and calm,
A skipped lunch.
You watched me grow
With a lazy, guarded eye
Like a cat, with less symmetry.
I cannot invent my face.
I cannot invent the yeasty, lipidous layer
That stopped moving long after I did.
Or the brittle shapes that
Threw themselves
Against the window
When gently,
'You don't have to do this anymore'
Would have sufficed.
So, surviving in this rancid bubble
A mix of chocolate cake and fear,
The days turn into years
And I live it
Wholly, fully, Completely.
Whilst obsequious armies
Revolve around you-
No doubt there are
Always two sides! (so they say)
But the smell
Of the greasepaint,
The roar of the crowd
Is all you can remember.

"Coda"
I run like in my dreams
And we move along
Beside the lemon tree
Where I write your song
But as I sit on my seat of stone,
I am licking my battle wounds.
A slave to your kingdom of hearts?
No.
I'll still find me somewhere,
Wherever I am.
When grass turns to snow,
What epic adventures,
Speeding home.
Hands off the wheel, foot off the brake,
And God,
What a brilliant year
Without you here.
Nursing my sores through paper straws.
Ice cream,
The sea,
And me.

2

"Classified"
Tall, blonde, gorgeous...
Seeking something sane.
Wanted-Disco dancing
And singing in the rain.
Let's see,
I'm drawn to northern lights,
Long walks in wellies,
Movie nights.
Please don't cut my roses,
I bleed out on their thorns
And don't bring me sunshine
I've been terribly burned before
Actually,
I'm a redhead now,
And I wear it up but it's ok,
I had gifts.
I over-egg the pudding
Over creamer
Over thinker.
I said, DON'T DO THAT AGAIN
He said, it's ok
He let me back in.
I blame the blame

The beautiful game
No fortune,
Just mess.
Payment in kind
And the rambling of a Madwoman
No attic left behind.
I over-egg the pudding
Over creamer, over thinker
Over dreamer, over stinker
Over beater, over drinker,

I sleep too loud

Over dreamery, over thinkery
Over
Over drink
Me.
My life in three bags-
Apply within.

BY: JESSICA LYON-WALL

"Ghost"
I am a blackbird woman
I tremble in the rain,
But I sit at your window.
I'm the sign of things to come.

I am a blackbird woman,
I trap your thoughts inside.
The root cause of morning
Is where I hide.

I am a ghost.
Oh, the faces of yours I have seen
Pull me to Earth,
Like gravity
And skin.

I know full well
What the end could be.
I know full well what the end could be.

I am a monster
I tie you to my moor
And more,
It's all I deserve, after all.

I am a Madwoman,
What I have seen
Is a dream short of sleep,
And what could have been.

"I Stumble, I Stand"
I stumble, I stand,
And hang my head.
My hands are tied.
A scene, a theme,
A unique piece of living art,
Pens clamped on the parts
that harbor my heart.

Mark my words,
I'll shake like a leaf
And succumb at first
To my beliefs, but slowly
I will unfurl like a shoot
From a stem.
I can't see them,
But I can feel them
Scribbling on the places that
No-one has yet reached.
Them, them, and their words all over my body.
You watch,
Carefully,
Quietly as it shivers in the moonlight
As I do, in the damp near-light.
I fall to my knees,
And you scoop up the tears I spill
At what I've learned.
Their words and your voice make up my mind,
I'll find peace in war,
Where words are kind.

BY: JESSICA LYON-WALL

"The Tower"
In the tower,
Him, the fool,
Wrapping in paper
Gifts of gold,
"I do," he whispered through merciless gloves,
Those Chinese messages
Were sent 'with love,'
And even on their wedding day,
He disappeared for two full hours,
Then jauntily, loudly,
Back he came,
Whilst she waited on a bed of blue,
Memories of past fertilities
Still rang true,
"Too much blood," she cried,
"And not enough said,
Not enough said,
M'Lord, in this cold hard bed,"
So, he left, you see,
For to find his way,
At least that's what the whispers say,
And whilst he stumbles through
Some foreign land,
To find another fair pale hand,
He dines out noisily on rumors, his,
Of how she placed a poisoned kiss,
Yet this we know, there is one 'truth'.
(It is hers that will prevail, for,
The man that sold
Her stories is the hero of his own tale!)

"I Am"
I am
Perfectly formed
And silver bound,
I part the golden nectar,
And have my handle in
Your hand.
I scoop and hold
Food in my belly,
Then give it
Up willingly,
Like a caress
On your lips.
I have
Hips that curve gently
Supine for soup!
The
Sting
Is
In
My
Tail.
That
You
Have
Found,
But
Then
I
Lose
My
Edges,
Unashamedly

BY: JESSICA LYON-WALL

Round.

3

"The Middle of the Bed"
The strange bones I kept
Before you came beside me
The day I ran wrong
Then you unwrapped me like a gift

Trapped inland
I would quietly drift
I lay in my song
You invited me to sit

As I threw off sparks
Between the fire and the sea
You said, 'Good Morning, Beautiful.
What will be, will be.'

I stood up straight
On the wrong side
Now the middle of the bed
Is where I hide

In case of an ending
I packed clothes too small
He lit the touch paper

BY: JESSICA LYON-WALL

And watched me burn

So,
I lay in my song
Invited to fit
The days I ran
You unwrapped me like a gift, and

I threw off sparks
Between land and sea
You said, 'Goodnight, Beautiful.
What will be, will be.'

"Siren"
I jump for
Fear of falling,
I swim for fear I drown.
I live for fear of leaving,
I'm the day's fateful sound.

I shine for
fear of burning,
go out and catch your eye.
The sea is coldly greasy,
A mouth where we align.

I sing for
Fear of silence,
I dream for fear I sleep.
I sit for fear of standing,
Oh,
The secrets that I keep.

I breathe for
Fear of choking,
I roam for fear I stay.
I can't dance,
A beauteous statue,
When hips are made of clay.

I weep for fear of laughing,
An unease inside me,
That you, I,
And the tumbling waves
Were never meant to be.

BY: JESSICA LYON-WALL

I sing
For fear your silence
Will haunt me as I sleep.
You, me,
And the tumbling seas
Were never meant to be.

"Cobalt"
Not ashen skin but skin ashes-
I shed like a snake as I take to the sky.
Black and blue,
White.
Not a raven,
But a magpie.
I'm glossy and coiffed,
Exuding energy yet existing singly.
I have lost my mate.

A trinity of colour, a master of none,
Yet I live.

BY: JESSICA LYON-WALL

"Serenity"
There's no breath in angels,
Or the recklessness of water.
I rip up my seventh step
And dance on the parts that God cannot reach.

"The Width of the World"
Hey, I got back.
I saw thousand and thousands of things,
I heard the thunder
Of the train through a nowhere station

...And the people
Who give me hundreds and hundreds of rings
All the silver,
The string-alongs, the weight of a nation.

Summer arrived,
The sun browned my skin and freckled my face
In a different place
To you.

Unruly hours
For months and weeks and days
I lived beyond my means
In many difficult ways.

In a white dress,
Lying on your conscience like a battered wife.
Still crazy.
In a moment, it will make me the

World's width,
When I looked through your eyes.
It's not different,
It's all I can see.

4

"...And Then"
Love's waiting at the gate, pensive, restless,
silent
Like a shell toe-top with secrets,
A box of delights.

Love's playing me a tune,
An Opera, an Aria,
A little night music.

Love's making me warm.
Thawing my bones, designing my flesh,
Desiring me.

Love's demanding to be felt,
Hard, surprised shivers.
A secret look, a starry eye,
Seeking permission to be let in.

"I Have Loved"
I have loved
Beyond my means
I am cut at the seams
I have
Enjoyed too little
And spent too much
I will have a little luck
I think
You are here
You will make the scars
Join with fear
I guess
This is what it's like
In the end
You would never strike out
So
I have loved
Beyond my means
I am broken at the seams
At least I have loved
At least
I have loved.

BY: JESSICA LYON-WALL

"A Train Journey"
Passing flooded fields that ripple and glitter,
The sun is unsure on his blustery day,
As girls with skirts that flip and sway
Grip on tightly with all their might,
Produce their tickets, then alight.
The train jolts heavily, then is spurred on
By engines humming thick and fast.
A church steeple interrupts a herd,
Animals hunch against each other ,
Cold and alert.

"The Boathouse"
Take me to my lover, so,
And send him home to me.
He's books on guns inside his hands
And I would set him free.

Oh bring me to the boathouse
So I can smell the sea
Oh bring me to the boathouse
And I would set him free.

I'll spin a yarn and truth like this
Hold tight onto my keys
And when I come to find him
He'll need a place to sleep.

Oh bring me to the boathouse
For he is kind to me,
Oh bring me to the boathouse
He'll need a place to sleep.

Unwind my traps and shackles, foe,
Then tie me up some more.
Of heroes that I read about
I liked him best of all.

Oh bring me to the boathouse
So I will never fall,
Oh bring me to the boathouse
I liked him best of all

Before I saw him singing,
I couldn't go that far.

BY: JESSICA LYON-WALL

From hospitals back home again
To where the sirens start.

Oh bring me to the boathouse
And never break my heart,
Oh bring me to the boathouse
To where the sirens start

Don't come too close, my tongue is tied
I cannot be alone.
And find himself inside my head
Of that he'll never know.

Oh bring me to the boathouse,
We'll have somewhere to go
Bring me to the boathouse
Of that he'll never know.

Oh bring me to the boathouse
So I can smell the sea.
He brings me to the boathouse,
For he is kind to me.

"Sixteen years of Winter"
I wrote it way back,
When all that I could see was
An empty bottle
In the damp, damp dark.
I dared myself the company.
Open the door, my friend!
It's getting cold out here.
Sixteen years of winter
Won't make you disappear.
There were times,
Do you remember?
We came out laughing,
Dancing hand in hand,
We would have
The strangest of evenings,
And exit stage left-to the sand!
I kept it shhh, a secret.
The illuminated lights went out once a season
Where we met in the cold,
Where I slept one Friday night.
(For we didn't know
That we'd be apart
When the time came
To really lose heart)
Coveting your colour,
You don't sing to me anymore.
I'm inland, in trouble.
Winter has been our enemy.
(Overnight,
A garish blanket
Stretched across the slumbering land.
Our trembling friends aren't

BY: JESSICA LYON-WALL

Making amends,
It's only us that make it to safety.
You sit on the pier,
I sip on a beer and breathe in
The thin, salty air.
You talk of love lost and love gained,
And how we remained friends
Through the years,
As I sit and wait for tomorrow)

5

"Eye Contact"
As it stands
I think you'll find me
With sour breath
On the bathroom floor
A clumsy oaf
Straight into doors

Lazily making
My way to the underworld
Neither here
Nor there
Nor really
Anywhere

As it stands
I will not be shaken anymore
'Till the next time

I don't remember
Affairs
The rage tattooed on your face
When you found out I knew,
And dear God,

BY: JESSICA LYON-WALL

The stairs

As it stands
I will not be shaken anymore
'Till the next time,
I'm fine.
I'll always be fine.

I wrap my hands
Around my house
The blooming roses
The marching weeds
The lowering sky,
Andullen seed.
Sullen.
Seed.
Sullen.
Seed.

Doubt creeps in
I have mighty claims
Not my child
In glinting frames
As it stands
I will not be shaken anymore
And crouch and hide behind old pine doors.

"If I Knew"
I'd liken this to a dream,
This, my love,
If I knew.
Stretched out and pristine.
Her skin under your hands
At best, yes,
If I knew.
Your poison acquiring the air
With nothing left to do.
You used to sing for me.
Now I steer straight and true
Ghosts in the boathouse,
Waiting, pulsating,
As if I knew.
I would wait under a bridge
Under a deep sigh of truths,
Your lies
Like vipers to my breast
And yes, this love,
If I knew.

BY: JESSICA LYON-WALL

"Weight"
In time, in time
The things on the walls that crawl
Will draw out the bones of us
As I choke out words in rhyme.
We couldn't budget for my heather
So you got them all to pray for me
Like a sickly old lady.

Dear you,
I'd write another
But I fear we're out of time,
'Cos you don't mess with tradition (amen)
I walked past the flowers,
The ones with Purple Hearts,
Stems that kept me safe.

Awake is not really asleep
When asleep is only half-right.
I dealt out my world card for you,
But was only shuffling time.
And your weight of the world,
There for those to admire
Whilst I floundered and left warning signs

I sit on your shoulders
So heavy you would fall
Bent at right angles and
Round as a wrecking ball

I picked my hands as you picked me apart.

I wish I could

But I'd run slow
They said I could
But I didn't go.
I promise tonight,
I'm jumping first.
No cages,
I grow to fit them.

So tired now, dreaming.
It's close.

I'm getting better at
Organizing your monsters.
A small child blowing bubbles in your steam.

So, I won't lend, and I won't borrow,
I won't beg and I won't steal,
Or tie anyone else in ribbon,
And finally, I'll sleep.

BY: JESSICA LYON-WALL

"An Unkindness of People"
I ask this sometimes,
With seas unkind
Why so sad?
Sea, sea, rewind, rewind.

Woods a dark hue fill
With acrid smoke,
An orange heart that burns with life
And takes it grandly, quickly,
Whilst high-end politicians
Talk loudly, to cameras,
On the streets where they wear blue.
But they just watch, and wait,
As we burn too..

We've starved our bodies
Like we starve the Earth
We scour the ground
For glittering gains
Drilling, draining
The shelter from rebelling rain

Cracks form in ground
That once was well,
Washed in waste
Their bellies swell

I sit on a pier, sip on some wine
And breathe in the thin salty air.
Oh! The things we could do,
If we dared.

Trees arch their backs over the narrow roads,
the cheering crowds go wild!

My Lancashire, my red rose home.
I would fall and kiss the ground
But I know it's not my own.

All we do is wait,
As if we had a choice,
But we do.
We have a voice.

BY: JESSICA LYON-WALL

"Mum's Net"

They mop up the bad ones,
These examples of motherhood
They gamely feed and
Cloth nappy their darlings,
Give birth in the woods.
They make their own bread and chew on the yeast,
And on the tip of their body
Is a poisonous breast.
A lash of a tongue, to the struggling ones,
The girls who don't sleep,
Up watching over the young.
The girls who can't eat,
As when they look away,
Toddlers
Toddle, towards the edge of the bay,
To paddle
Unsupervised, unstoppable,
Unwavering, and senseless
With
little fat legs,
The waves
lap on their toes.
Mother blinks as she reaches for ice cream,
To treat her young girl
The waves
Lapping deeper,
And a web starts to uncurl
Of other young mothers,
Who watch with a stare
But sit and do nothing-
Paddlers beware!

They whisper and
Twitter like
Owls on the crack
Watch as the baby falls, will she ever come back?
And before mum can clock danger
A hero
Appears,
And seals with a kiss the fate of mum,
With a hiss.
A brief silence falls on the web,
They cheer like fans, then rage t'wards mum
She turns and the fear of God's on her face,
Her last saved, scrimped,
Suddenly dropped pound in her hand.

6

"Skin-Tight"
I can hear the birds already,
I'm beginning to begin,
As it's so far from last night
It's only 5am.

Whispers started days ago
Cracks are forming, wide,
As my mind takes flight
To skin-tight.

As 7 comes and goes,
I pull on earthly clothes
That are looser than before.
They smell like yesterday.

We never know to stop,
It only comes and goes
Like a feather, to skin-tight,
To skin-tight.

I'll blow you away,
My stories are foul whispers
That linger in the dawn

Where they were.

There is no excuse
At 4am,
Reaching out in the yard,
To skin-tight.

I watch the bubbles rise
And my heart sinks.
Just another glass of water,
Sticks and stones.

You talk of anger
I talk of rage.
A shook-up can of cola,
Unmarked page.

I can hear the birds already.
I'm beginning to begin,
And it's so far from last night,
It's only 3am.

BY: JESSICA LYON-WALL

"Consumption"
They joined in,
The ones who knew about
Shades of black and white.
We made unhappy music from
Inside a grinning shell.
The fabric was brittle
And lacy
Against transparent skin
And glaring red lines.

We turned our faces to the sun,
Needing everything,
Wanting nothing,
Asking nothing.

"You Said, You Said"
You said everything, 'I do,'
Means everything to you
And it's all fine.

You told me that the air
Would fill my lungs again,
It was all mine!

Now you say we burned out
Like stars in the sky
I'm not sure that it's true
I'm not sure that you're right.
And I'm not sure that I wrote
The lines around your eyes
By gaslight

Words rumble far away
Now I stay beside the sea
I can only hope,

That the more I pick-
The less it bleeds-
That it won't snow.

Now you say we burned out
Like stars in the sky.
I'm not sure that it's true,
I'm not sure that you're right.
And I'm not sure that I wrote
The lines around your eyes
By gaslight.

BY: JESSICA LYON-WALL

And I had not slept

For promises I kept
The way you talk.

I just can't concentrate
There are things You said I'd done
Only you saw

So you said we burned out
That you'd discovered why
Reckoned you'd take flight
Like a raven in the sky.
I'm not sure that I wrote
The lines around your eyes
I don't think that I saw
The lines around your eyes
By gaslight.

"Broken Hill"

Final truths and songs un-played
Places where we loved and laid.
Memories, if nothing else
Bring sweaty palms and Sundays, blessed.

My mind's sharp metre that you stole,
An ill-divining, restless soul.
And fireworks, noisy lights,
Diamonds for forever, bright.

Holding breath, and turning blue
I remember, And I burn too
You made me walk on my tiptoes
Now we can't dance, I weep and moan.

My eyes were heavy when you spoke
Of lullabies, the things you'd done
You said 'here is me, it's history,
I made my name beside the sea.'

I should not have listened, nor have stayed
Left empty promises in their grave
'Cos as you whispered of your past,
Said 'I'll be yours while Autumn lasts.'

You once mentioned Northern lights
But said, there'll be a sacrifice.
'Your dress is chosen, and if I may,
The book to bring a judgement day.'

Even motorways, the ice's edge

BY: JESSICA LYON-WALL

Did not stir the day you left
And as I slept, the cold spell broke,
You didn't even leave a note.

I want to turn the world a hue
Of words, and wisdom, silent blues,
And destiny, and barefoot grass,
Then finely, finally, I'll dance.

And destiny, and barefoot grass,
Then finely, finally, I'll dance

"Flagship"
It's ok going
Partway
When your frame fits the door,
But we're rough around the edges,
A boathouse but no shore.
I danced and drank and slept with lions,
Now I can't dream anymore,
But it's ok that your frame doesn't fit
When there's a boathouse but no shore.

And it's ok you're a limbo,
'Cos it's all that's left of me.
My lovers were a flagship divided by the sea.
Skin the oldest papers,
Stretched out and obscene,
And though standing inches taller,
I sink from wild to meek.

I sought a group to wreck,
A town to cause affray.
The candle burned all night for me
From place to place,
And had a mind to mending
When every night was day.
You put the breath in castles
To keep the ghosts away.

How kind to pick the pieces
Of a part that's yet to break!
How tender were the wolves in ordinary ways.
You came quietly,
Shifting shape to stem,

BY: JESSICA LYON-WALL

Unbending as the statues
Of ordinary men.

7

"Cigarette"
When upon her lips
In red, your name
My lonely dreams
Mean a lonely day.

Which I thought first
And you said the same-
A knight alone is a knight in vain

Higher than
Thin salty air
Now this hurts more
Then that did there,

Ran down the dunes
For a broken dare-
Broken hearts for a child's nightmare

So, I was not
The only hand
That held yours tight,
Made you a man.

BY: JESSICA LYON-WALL

'She is better off
Alone and sad.'
They whisper at night, because they can

At the brittle snow
I stood and wept
You use up souls
Like a cigarette

Which we stopped at

The store to get-
A moonlit night is a night ill-met.
A moonlit night is a night ill-met.

"Astonishing Lightness"
They made promises
I got so few
Promises like this.

Stale in a mouth
Green with envy
Pale with anger you must
Defend a right to live.

There should have been
Seven stages of men, but I got two,
Mewling and puking
Crippled too
Words mean nothing now
I talk to myself
They were my weakness and
They were my health

The books say, 'hysterical woman,'
But I reckoned to wealth,
Strong and careful
With astonishing lightness,

Carrying the remains
Of past fertilities
I think my story rings true
To everyone but you.

It isn't my song, after all

BY: JESSICA LYON-WALL

"Grandma's Footsteps"
Still there, counting the wires.
I can't get in and I can't get out.
Knees deep in bodies
Scattered on the floor,
ICU
ICU
I see you.
The high that never climbs
The dreams that will not die
I served no God's,
No monsters,
Was the moon that made me wide,
Wide,
Wide.
The smile on my face
At midnight dark
The front seat best spot nothing
But flight
the black sheep gut-
Rot last door to the right.
I haven't found a size to fit me yet, bite, bite,
Don't bite.

"I waited for Water"
The draw of water
Anchors bones
So dry we
Can't walk at all.
Wretched and bent
Without air
The fear
Of wanting to fall

Reach me
On the narrow road
With my cold
And restless skin.
I'll feel you, Lord,
With fuller heart
And find the light
Within.

I would move from land
And rivers
To Seas,
The places!
My body tired,
Yet a quiet noise
On the wind
On the page.

Lead me
To this narrow road.

BY: JESSICA LYON-WALL

"So much to tell you"
Broken, and willing.
Drunken, and singing.
The last time I said,
'I'll do this tomorrow.'

Crowd it with something,
I dream more than I sleep,
And run until it hurts
On a splintering knee.

Oh Alice, you grew so small
Bones push against your skin
Now who knows who will win?

An old wooden bench,
In the middle of town,
Near a graveyard of secrets,
My bread falls to the ground.

Stared out the window,
The glass I painted,
Pills lined up like soldiers
I kept on my tongue.

Whispers and talking
Too loud to be heard.
I crept to my room,
And ate up their words.

Oh Alice, you grew so small
Bones push against your skin

Now who knows who will win?

The dot dot hydrochloride
Would dull the rumblings
Of a crazy...
Alice, you grew
Alice, you grew
Alice, you grew,
Alice you grew, Oh,
Alice, eat me drink me-
There's so much to tell you!

It's all in the pages,
Very much like night,
I'd put it in a letter-
There isn't time.

8

"The Colour of Love"
My mum said, 'three's an ugly number.'
For once, she was right.
I hold my ring in palms gone blue
And my hair is growing white.

She said, 'don't trust that man.
Nor assume he'll not bite.'
Teeth marks fade to purple
And in whore's beds he lies

Said, 'don't hold him up, too.
You'll collapse under the weight.'
Still, I need a warning.
I'm counting down my days.

My spring skin turns warm and pink
My clothes closer to pale.
I think I have a calling,
But it's him, calling late.

I throw my ring in trash turned
Brown,
For once, she was right.

(I think I had a calling, for,
He always called at night)

I still sleep with one eye open
Trained towards yellow night
I still sleep with the lamp on
I sleep, I'm never right.

I can't sleep, the dark is mine
He stole my light and days
How did I love him?
Let me count the waves.

She said, 'three is an ugly number.'
For once, she was right.
I hold my heart in palms gone blue
And my hair is turning white.

BY: JESSICA LYON-WALL

"Sheepcountwolves"
I stood in your lightbox,
You saw every part of me.
The past is passed
What will be,
Will be.

Don't be scared, love.
We are two desperate sides
Wrapped around our truths, where we hide.

I still have nightmares,
I know you do.
And when they can't sleep,
Sheep count wolves.

We're years older, I have lines
On my skin
Still scared of the shadows, and
What they may bring,

BUT this I know,
(Now I'm firmly on the ground)
I'll still be singing
As the world falls down.
Don't push too far ahead
I loved you on an empty stomach
My skin cracks and peels
As I reach out

I stood in your light box
You saw every part of me

Worlds apart

My back to the wall

Breath is a choice
So I held mine
Stay or breathe, truth or dare
I keep my bones everywhere.

Safe in my glass
'Till I saw me through yours
The sky clouded up
The boats bent their oars

Breath is a choice
So I held mine
Stay or breathe, truth or dare
I keep my bones everywhere

See, they were asymmetrical
Too bent for you break
Now I can't find you
In my lonely state

Death is a voice
So I fed mine.
Breath is a choice
So I held mine
Stay and dream, truth or dare
I keep my bones
Everywhere.

BY: JESSICA LYON-WALL

"Ev'ry Hill"

I shout your name from ev'ry hill
To find out where you hide
I shout your name from ev'ry hill
To make you come outside.

I sing of seas and black-winged birds
That tremble as they fly
The mighty and the man absurd
Will that make you come outside?

I talk of love and thickened dawns
Greased salty air and seas
A wretch, the cause of morning
When I'm awake at three

Night-time comes, a steady stream
Of wandering memories
I filter out the treasure chest
To keep the ones I need

So here I am, on beds of stone
With evening's fateful stare.
Godspeed my love, I hope you find
Her gone in thin, cold air!

"Party Animal"
The ways I swayed!
They tipped a wink
A nod
A drink
It may be Sunday,
But when they look away
I still dance
Broken puppet limbs,
Marks from lovers past
I hope they're shaking,
My joints are aching from running too fast
Still we do it,
We get roses
But pricked by the thorns wear the red like a badge,
'Look what you did!
You must be more careful.'
A dear, sweet thing.
Black and blue under the skin.
Wading, not living, in want
Of nothing.

The ways I stayed.
They tipped a wink,
And I when I blinked,
A drink.
It may be someday,
But when they look away, I'll dance.

"Don't"
Don't be scared, love.
We are two desperate sides
Wrapped around this faith
Where we can hide.

Don't look behind love,
No good lies there, though
He left like a breath
In the thick warm air.

So hold me now, take me in,
And it's that simple,
Lying low in the north,
The things we used to do
For fear of getting caught.

Listen, here's a secret,
Where else would I be?
The tides have turned, he made me burn,
You put me out in the blue-green sea.

You found madness of your own,
In the years that passed.
You left your heart 'till last.
We left our hearts 'till last.

9

"Goodbye Ruth Elizabeth"
It was in the tall, tall reeds
Eyes resting on the glare,
It was night-time by the river
I'm sure I saw you there

So, if it really matters,
I don't know what to say,
But Goodbye Ruth Elizabeth.
It's sometimes
Morning all day.

The aching got me first,
So close! And not too far,
No longer by the water,
Inland, inside the grass.

All I do is watch
And wait, for
It was long.
It got late,

Or if you really matter,
I don't know what to say, but,

BY: JESSICA LYON-WALL

Goodbye Ruth Elizabeth,
It's sometimes
Morning all day.

Can't breathe.
Can't speak.
Can't even hear a heartbeat.
I just look,

And wait.

If it even matters,
I don't know who to blame,
Goodbye Ruth Elizabeth,
It's always
Morning all day.

Bye-bye.
You were only
An idea
After all.
Anyway.

"Conscience"
Now it's much too much
Lying next to you
Would it be the roses
Wilting too
That pricked your conscience?
Or the broken ornaments,
Or the ripping of paper alas no,
It's the sound of the door
Soft click on a latch as I screw my courage
And leave the key behind this time.
Only let it be said,
You walked away first.

I used to think it was lucky,
Getting what you want
Now it's much too much
Lying next to you, it just is
Much too much.
Sickly stench of roses
Edges brown and gaunt
Is it your conscience
Wilting too,
Your conscience wilting too.
I hope you come back
Back to where I keep the truth.

Just us,
And alone
And words
And the secrets I never tell
For fear of letting go
The places I will go! For fear of getting caught

BY: JESSICA LYON-WALL

Why I walk with my head down
All the bitterness that breaks
The energy it takes

The soft click
Of the latch as I screw my courage
And leave the key this time.
Just let it be said
You walked away first.

"You Know I'm Right"

I would bow and scrape
To your male sensibilities,
If I thought it would get me anywhere.

I find it astounding that in this day and age
We are still silenced by power, like a
Cyber scold's bridle.

And you brought disaster,
But who would believe me anyway?
You gladly speak to your acquaintances
About how you had me on the bathroom floor,
And used the back of your hand
To shut me up.

I am quiet now, the authorities
Were not interested
In my wailing's
And bouts of hysterical laughter, so,
I am sore.
Perhaps I did want it, after all.

BY: JESSICA LYON-WALL

"Dear Sir"
Thank you for your correspondence,
Further to your email, regarding my divorce,
The thoughts behind it, and the petition
Are set out below,
And will outline my decision.

You see, he saw me play guitar one day,
The rest, as they say
Is history, but the mystery remains,
Why?
How did we go from here to there?
Not that but this, not really anywhere.

THIS IS WHAT YOU'VE DONE!!!!!!!!!!

Clears throat (quietly)
Further to your email, regarding my divorce,
One has made up one's mind,
I would rather have a horse.

Yours sincerely.
Scorned of Manchester

"Viper"
The things that go by
In the loneliest hour

What horrors are expressed in the night!
Lavish killings, sky-clad rituals,
Tainted lovers and angry wives
Whose hearts thump with fear
Behind pale moonlight.

I used to stand in the yard and write, and hear
The planes land safely, out of sight.

My cigarette smoke curled into acrid tails,
Like a viper to my lungs,
I didn't care.
My stomach complained bitterly,
Too hungry to eat
My mind a whirling
Complete with grief.

You slept soundly, you always did,
Your machine clicked and whirred
Like an anxious pig.
I've no doubt you dreamt sweetly,
After milk and prayers,
As I pushed make-believe prams
And pulled out my hair.

9 nights, once, fueled by pills
And it got strange, as if I was ill,
Because
I was the mad one, who would wail and weep,

BY: JESSICA LYON-WALL

I was the one

Who could not sleep.
You were the one I could not call
And sometimes I wonder whether
I was ever there
At all.

10

"Old Blood"
We need to talk. We need to fix
This blurred line, these pick-up sticks.
I went there- if I had known the way the wind blows!
I got small
To be the same.
I went to the hospital
But they never came.

The baffling wilderness that I crashed through
As elegant trees arched their backs
Over narrow roads
I used every breath available
To hinder their view.
I took the back streets home from dance, and
Went from enormous,
Beautiful mirrors and me,
Making nasty,
Gnarly shapes with gargantuan hands.
Hands that later
I shoved down my throat
To gag up what little I consumed.

An apple a day didn't keep the doctors away.

BY: JESSICA LYON-WALL

They came one after the other in a skinny line,
Promising enticing delicacies if only
I would let them make me fatter.
I wear my flesh
Like armor,
But that year I had none
And the memories of schoolgirls past
Floated by carelessly.
Every night on those pale green corridors.
They haunt me by smell, by taste, by touch,
Like ferrous nails down an old blackboard.
So ghosted I could not sleep,
I put my midnight head on,
Pushing food around a plate
Like a demented rodent,
And being yelled at for having too much,
For being too thin-
I could never win. I could never win.

I don't live there anymore.
The streets where they wear blue are miles and
miles away

And to this day I seek them out.
I pick up the penny
That I found
It went so fast
And was so loud.

"Liar Liar"
He fed me, early on,
With his velvety words
He brought me a beautiful crystal
Raped from Mother Earth.

It snowed that first Winter
Foot on foot of powdery dread.
I looked on and saw all this,
All this is good, I said.

He played me songs of valor
Of heroes far and wide,
Ditties from his own fair hand,
Liar, liar, pants on fire.

(He ground my bones
Into a thick kind of vapor,
As I watched, beguiled, reached
For my inhaler.

He put poison in my coffee
Spread hatred on my bread)

I saw all this, and meant it,
'It is good,' I said.

One day in October, Halloween, to be precise,
I bound myself in satin,
In a sheath of pure white.
But as I limped down the aisle,
His face set with a frown.

BY: JESSICA LYON-WALL

It was the wrong day for this, maybe

I should have been a shroud.

He wanted a baby,
But no babies came
Each month
I cried on the toilet,
Each one was the same.
So I pulled
My insides out,
And wrapped them,
Like a prize,
Whilst my outside rotted down to
An unearthly, scaly size.

Bedtime's cavernous mouth gaped-
There came no sleep.
2am in the snow in thick green boots
The bridge seemed like a relief.

And still, months later,
I danced by the light of the moon,
For when stars got full-
It meant he'd be back soon.

The fields, I knew, were singing.
Moments later, I was dead,
I arose, not seeing or knowing.
It is good, I said.

"On cleaning an oven"
Lying the colour
Of my finger,
And twice as thick,
Oblivious to trained under-the-sink condiments
It is a harbor of poison acquiring the air,
Drifting through
Door cracks in increments;
Greasy, ordered
Like Satan's army of hamburger stands,
Of forgotten entities,
And cursing its malevolence
And the impossibility of the task,
I light my candles on the gas ring and
Thank God for the toaster.

BY: JESSICA LYON-WALL

"My Body"
I fear my armor
I need it too,
It stretches over me, a porcelain mantle,
And colours my insides blue.
(Like skin, it has had many uses
Though it dimples, bruises, itches, and oozes,
Though it has seen a thousand things,
The terror has not changed once)
A so-called love that thawed my bones
Whilst I designed my flesh
I told him no cages, that I grow to fit,
But he nailed me down anyway
In rooms unlit.
Don't tell me
That the largest heart
Is of a man!
Who's wrestling limbs shall cover mine
My chamber will change your mind!
The rest was silence,
But my stomach growled
Angry and forgotten,
And my cuts, though freshly remembered
Bled dry from within.
Now.
Now I fill a room with a hundred ghosts
Of the person I thought I knew, or was.
This could be too the last thing I write,
But you stay on my mind,
Rotting memories that retch and writhe
Like I did, down a mountainside.
Love?
Love is for fools,

And we're all fools

I fear my armor,

But I need it too.

BY: JESSICA LYON-WALL

"Behind the Arras"

Be you and I behind an arras then,
Whispering half-truths in the twilight,
Backs sliding along the sand, laughing
The shattering of glass masking our screams
With flowers in our hair.
I tried to distract you
From the blank canvass of your skin
I tried to console you from the madness within.
We spent too long staring into the smoke
And whiled away the hours.
I thought you were beside me
You were dragged away by fate
We talked of nothing and ate
Nothing.
What a tragic turn of events.
I didn't mean to unwind
My tapestry at your little feet.
But so be it.
You're here now.
We walk carefully
And quietly, we don't kiss,
We say,
'let's talk about this, and this, and this'

Photo By:
Jessica Lyon-Wall

Jessica wrote a poem about a boy in 1994 at age 14. She subsequently won the school poetry prize. Her love for words started at a very young age, and she was always writing stories, poems and songs...occasionally in her school books. This led to a diploma in Performing Arts, where she discovered her love for singing and playing guitar.

Jessica formed the duo, 'All My Ghosts', and gigged original music in the Greater Manchester area until 2018, releasing an album, single, and EP. Following the deterioration of her arthritis she turned to poetry again when it became too painful to play guitar.

Jessica's work is an intimate portrait of relationships, healing and life with chronic illness and mental health conditions. Although painful, it is uplifting and above all else always honest. Her influences include Carol Ann Duffy, Sylvia Plath and Virginia Woolf.

Jessica is in her final year of an English and Creative Writing degree, and is currently working on her first novel. She hopes her words will help other survivors of domestic abuse. Jessica lives in the North-West of England with her partner, son, and cat Dave.

Photo By:
Jessica Lyon-Wall

Photo By:
Jessica Lyon-Wall

Photo By:
Jessica Lyon-Wall

Photo By:
Jessica Lyon-Wall

Lightning Source UK Ltd.
Milton Keynes UK
UKHW051212231222
414235UK00013B/40